SPOTLIGHT
ON CHILDREN'S
AUTHORS

DR. SEUSS

DEBORAH

GRAHAME-SMITH

Cavendish
Square

New York

Published in 2015 by Cavendish Square Publishing, LLC
243 5th Avenue, Suite 136, New York, NY 10016

Website: cavendishsq.com

This publication represents the opinions and views of the author based on his or her personal experience, knowledge, and research. The information in this book serves as a general guide only. The author and publisher have used their best efforts in preparing this book and disclaim liability rising directly or indirectly from the use and application of this book.

CPSIA Compliance Information: Batch #WS14CSQ

All websites were available and accurate when this book was sent to press.

Library of Congress Cataloging-in-Publication Data

Grahame-Smith, Deborah.
Dr. Seuss / by Deborah Grahame-Smith.
p. cm. — (Spotlight on children's authors)
Includes index.
ISBN 978-1-62712-846-9 (hardcover) ISBN 978-1-62712-847-6 (paperback) ISBN 978-1-62712-848-3 (ebook)
1. Seuss, — Dr. — Juvenile literature. 2. Authors, American — 20th century — Biography — Juvenile literature.
3. Illustrators — United States — Biography — Juvenile literature. I. Grahame-Smith, Deborah. II. Title.

PS3513.E2 Z623 2015
813—d23

Editorial Director: Dean Miller
Editor: Andrew Coddington
Copy Editor: Sara Howell
Art Director: Jeffrey Talbot

Designer: Amy Greenan
Production Manager: Jennifer Ryder-Talbot
Production Editor: David McNamara
Photo Research: J8 Media

The photographs in this book are used by permission and through the courtesy of: Cover photo by John Bryson/TIME & LIFE Images/Getty Images; Gene Lester/Archive Photos/Getty Images, 4; Detroit Publishing Company/File:Main Street-Springfield, Massachusetts.jpg/Wikimedia Commons, 6; Keystone-France/Hulton Archive/Getty Images, 9; FPG/Archive Photos/Getty Images, 11; Art Phaneuf-LostArts/Shutterstock.com, 12; Dartmouth College Library, 14; Hulton Archive/Getty Images, 18; Naval Historical Foundation, 21; Gene Lester/Archive Photos/Getty Images, 23; © AF archive/Alamy, 25; Gene Lester/Archive Photos/Getty Images, 26; © Photo Researchers/Alamy, 28; Library of Congress, 30; Everett Collection/Newscom, 34; © Stan Tess/Alamy, 37; David Bjorgen/File:Seuss Landing.jpg/Wikimedia Commons, 38.

Printed in the United States of America

CONTENTS

INTRODUCTION:
A Story No One Can Beat

One wintery afternoon, Theodor "Ted" Seuss Geisel, the man who would become Dr. Seuss, walked on what turned out to be the lucky side of Madison Avenue in New York City. He carried the well-frayed, typed manuscript of his first children's book, *A Story That No One Can Beat*.

Ted was no stranger to the landmark route of designer shops and advertising firms. He was a successful political cartoonist for magazines and newspapers and a commercial artist for major accounts such as Essomarine motor oils and Flit bug spray. However, this book had hit a brick wall. After more than twenty rejections from publishers, Ted was ready to head to his apartment on Park Avenue and plan a fitting ritual to burn the relic of this dead-end chapter in his career as a quirky illustrator of original rhymes for kids.

At that time, a college friend, Mike McClintock, had just started a new job as a children's book editor for Vanguard

Press. Mike was walking on the same lucky side of the avenue on the same afternoon when he bumped into Ted. As they chatted, Mike asked Ted about the manuscript he was carrying. "Come on up and let's look at it," Mike said, and by the time Ted left Mike's office, he had a contract to publish the manuscript, now with a "snappier" title: *And to Think That I Saw It on Mulberry Street*. The boy in the story was renamed after McClintock's young son, and the book was dedicated to "Helene McC, Mother of the One and Original Marco."

The story began as far from the concrete canyons of New York City as can be imagined—on the rough seas during a turbulent crossing from Europe to the ports of New York. Ted passed the hours while others were secluded and seasick by navigating the decks and daydreaming to the rhythm of the mighty engines of the MS *Kungsholm*.

Ted disembarked from the ship with notes scratched on a yellow pad of paper. It took six months of tweaking and pondering the rightness of every word before he felt ready to present the manuscript to Manhattan publishers. Their swift, negative decrees took on a pattern of excuses: there was no lesson or moral; verse was out of fashion; and fantasy did not sell. Once Vanguard published the book, however, glowing notices in the *New Yorker*, the *Atlantic Monthly*, and the *New York Times* proved the naysayers wrong.

Ted later said that if he had been walking on the other side of Madison Avenue that afternoon, he would have gone into the dry cleaning business. Luckily for children everywhere, that never happened.

The Main Street of downtown Springfield, Massachusetts, just around the time that Theodor Geisel was born.

Chapter 1
THE BREWER'S KID WITH THE THREE-LEGGED DOG

Theodor Seuss Geisel was born in Springfield, Massachusetts, on March 2, 1904. Surrounded by his German-American parents and grandparents, aunts, uncles, and cousins, he grew up speaking both German and English. His older sister, Margaretha Christine, called "Marnie," was two years older. Their early years were spent at 22 Howard Street in downtown Springfield. Ted's family later settled at 74 Fairfield Street, where he lived from age four until he left for college. Ted's childhood companions included his Boston bull terrier, Rex, who walked on three of its four legs, and Theophrastus, the chubby, stuffed brown dog he kept nearly his whole life.

Ted's grandfather, also named Theodor, arrived in Springfield from the German territory of Baden in the nineteenth century. By the 1870s, he had established a brewery on Boston Road in Springfield with another young German immigrant, Christian Kalmbach. The Kalmbach & Geisel Springfield Brewery Company became a popular part of the community, with a production capacity of 1,000 barrels a year. By the time Ted's father, Theodor Robert Geisel, was a youngster in the 1880s, the brewery covered ten acres (4 hectares), and barrel capacity had jumped to a whopping 40,000 per year. Eventually Kalmbach & Geisel acquired the comical name "Come Back and Guzzle" among local patrons. The kind of word play that Dr. Seuss is known for seemed to be a part of his DNA.

Springfield at the turn of the twentieth century was a Yankee metropolis of factories, vaudeville companies, museums, and railroads. Authors and artists often sprinkle bits of their hometown into their work many years after they have left. Ted used memories of Springfield's parades, buildings, landscape, and common family names such as McElligot, Terwilliger, Wickersham, and Norval Bacon, into his drawings and rhymes. Ted's hometown nostalgia included the colorful characters who shared his street: the sober Bumps, who were disapproving of the Geisel family beer business, and the Italian Bondis, whose daughters were named Roma, Florence, and Venice. Mulberry Street was the main thoroughfare of the town, and was the setting of his first published children's book.

Ted learned to read when very young. His mother, Springfield native Henrietta Seuss Geisel (Nettie), read bedtime stories to Ted and Marnie in a soothing, rhythmic chant she learned when she sold pies in a bakery as a young girl: "Apple, mince, lemon... peach, apricot, pineapple... blueberry, coconut, custard, and SQUASH!" Years later, Ted credited his mother for inspiring him to create "the rhythms in which I write and the urgency with which I do it."

Nettie found that she could entice Ted to focus on his scheduled piano lessons in Springfield's Court Square with the promise of a book. If he did well, she took him to Johnson's Bookstore across the street and let him choose. Ted often picked a title from the Rover Boys series. *The Hole Book* (with a "bullet" hole on every page) by Peter Newell was an early favorite. The Goops books (tips on manners for "impolite infants") by Gelett Burgess, and Alice Raiker's *The Tootle Bird and the Brontos* were also likely to have been on Ted's shelves. *The Tootle Bird* featured beasts with names like the Snook and the Whiffle-Grub that could have migrated to a future Dr. Seuss menagerie.

When Ted was a bit older he devoured books by contemporary writer Hilaire Belloc, whose strange titles and rhythmic prose sparked the young artist's imagination: *The Bad Child's Book of Beasts*, *More Beasts for Worse Children*, and *Cautionary Tales for*

Like this boy, young Ted Geisel loved to read and would be rewarded for doing well at piano lessons with a trip to the bookstore for a new book.

Children. Fanciful illustrations by BTB (Lord Ian Basil Temple Blackwood) introduced Ted to the infinite artistic possibilities of imaginary animals.

When the Germans torpedoed the British ocean liner *Lusitania* in 1915, killing 128 Americans, it was no longer acceptable to be of German ancestry in Springfield—or in any American town for that matter. Almost overnight, neighbors who were once friendly turned sour toward the Geisels. Ted heard from a friend that he was known as "the German brewer's kid with the three-legged dog." When the United States entered World War I two years later, anti-German sentiment was at a fever pitch in many American cities. Springfield was no exception, despite its heavy German-American population of about 1,200 adults and 5,000 children. Springfield libraries emptied their shelves of German books. Sauerkraut was renamed "liberty cabbage," and frankfurters were to be called "hot dogs" according to a congressional committee.

Ted entered high school in the fall of 1917 and took just one art class before being told that breaking the rules of artists would lead to failure. He dropped the class. At age 14, Ted joined the war effort, collecting used tin foil, selling war bonds, and growing a two-acre victory garden of potatoes. He forgot to harvest the potatoes, but he earned an award for being among the top ten in war bond sales from his Boy Scout troop. Marnie and Nettie, meanwhile, knitted blankets and socks for American GIs.

The family's booming beer business went bust in 1920 with the start of Prohibition, which banned the manufacture and sale of all

ONE TED, TWO TED...

Ted Geisel, top-ten seller of war bonds, waited to receive his Boy Scout award with nine other scouts onstage at Springfield's Municipal Auditorium, facing an audience of thousands of locals. Former U.S. president Theodore Roosevelt bestowed the medals, pausing for the salute of each scout and the resulting applause, until he reached young Ted. There were no more medals on the table, and the elder Ted inquired in a booming voice, "What's this little boy doing here?" The scoutmaster hustled Ted offstage without explaining the error, and Ted suffered the rest of his life with a paralyzing stage fright that prevented him from television interviews and speeches when he became a world-famous author.

alcoholic beverages in the United States. The Geisel beer dynasty may have collapsed, but the family's real estate holdings and other investments kept them afloat during Ted's high school years. Ted's father eventually became trustee, and then head of, Forest Park, which included the Forest Park Zoo. He kept this position well into his eighties. One day the Seussian Springfield of feasts and beasts would be reimagined in the drawings and words of its native son.

Theodor Geisel attended Dartmouth College, an Ivy League school in Hanover, New Hampshire.

Chapter 2

ON BEYOND SPRINGFIELD

Ted entered Dartmouth College in Hanover, New Hampshire, in the fall of 1921. A young high school English teacher, Edwin A. "Red" Smith, fresh out of Dartmouth himself, had encouraged Ted to apply to the Ivy League institution. As in high school, Ted endured just a single art class, during which he argued with his teacher about the concept of balance. "The teacher wanted me to draw the world as it was," Ted explained. "I wanted to draw things as I saw them."

Because Ted's classmates assumed the freshman with the German surname and black hair was Jewish, he was not invited to pledge a fraternity. The isolation Ted felt led him to turn his talents to Dartmouth's humor magazine, the *Jack-O-Lantern* (nicknamed the *Jacko*), and the school newspaper, the *Dartmouth*. Ted soon found a literary sponsor in sophomore Norman "Mac" Maclean, a minister's son from Montana. As editor-in-chief of the *Jacko*, Maclean helped Ted get some illustrations and lines published. Ted eventually became *Jacko* editor-in-chief himself. "My big desire was to run that magazine," Ted recalled years later. "If Mac hadn't picked me as his successor, my whole life at college would have been a failure."

Ted's lifelong love of fashionable clothing is evident in this portrait taken on the Dartmouth campus.

During Prohibition, smuggling bootleg alcohol was big business and a temptation to citizens and students alike. In his senior year, Ted was caught serving gin at a party in his dorm room, and he was banned from writing for the school paper and magazine. He continued to contribute cartoons and articles under various pseudonyms, including Ted Seuss, using his mother's maiden name.

Even though Ted was officially voted "least likely to succeed" by his Dartmouth classmates, he was regarded as a great wit and good company at any school event or party. "When he walked into a room it was like a magician's act," said fellow student Kenneth Montgomery. "Birds flew out of his hands, and endless bright scarves and fireworks. Everything became brighter, happier, funnier."

As graduation approached, Ted realized he had no clear career path, and he was not confident in his skills in language or art. "English and writing was my major," he reflected, "but I think that's a mistake for anybody. That's teaching you the mechanics of getting water out of a well that may not exist."

On a whim, and to keep the reality of adulthood at bay a little while longer, Ted decided to pursue graduate studies and enrolled at Oxford University, in England.

Ted arrived at Oxford's Lincoln College with a typewriter and a sense of expectation. This was where he intended to settle the question of whether he would become a writer, an artist, or a college professor of English Literature. In unexpected ways, this next year at Oxford would in fact shape his future and put his life into sharper perspective.

As always, Ted preferred sketching to studying, and he participated in campus life without exerting himself academically. His black loose-leaf notebook had margins filled with beguiling creatures, prototypes of characters that would one day appear in his books. Another American student, Helen Palmer, noticed these drawings during a class she shared with Ted. "You're crazy to be a professor," she told him after class. "What you really want to do is draw." Ted was smitten with this slim New Jersey girl with the light blue eyes, and they were immediately inseparable.

During Easter break, Ted toured Paris with Helen and her mother, and impulsively they got engaged. At the end of the spring term, Ted's tutor advised him to take a year-long break and broaden himself by traveling through Europe's cities, museums, and historical landmarks. That summer, Ted visited Switzerland and Germany with Marnie and his parents. He stayed on after the Geisels sailed back to the States. While Helen completed her studies at Oxford that fall, Ted meandered through Vienna, Paris, and Italy, where he reunited with Helen and her mother. By winter, both Helen and Ted were back in the States. Helen accepted a teaching job in New Jersey. Ted headed north to Springfield, determined to crank out humorous writings and drawings for submission to New York editors.

Months of silence and rejection passed, but in July Ted sold a cartoon to the *Saturday Evening Post* for twenty-five dollars. Ted believed that this sale was his life's turning point, and he promptly packed his bags for New York. After landing a job at the humor magazine *Judge*, Ted felt the time was finally right for him to marry Helen. The couple had a simple home wedding in November 1927, and settled in a rough New York neighborhood known as Hell's Kitchen.

In 1928, a Seuss cartoon in *Judge* mentioned the bug spray Flit, a Standard Oil Company product. The cartoon was brought to the attention of Flit's advertising firm, and Ted was signed on to a seventeen-year campaign whose slogan, "Quick, Henry, the Flit!" saturated popular culture. Ted's connection to Flit brought him work from magazines such as *Life* and *Vanity Fair*. He drew ads for General

Electric and NBC. Soon he was earning more money per year than his Dartmouth classmates with successful careers in law or banking.

Ted and Helen prospered during the Great Depression, moving to a better apartment on West End Avenue and traveling to more than thirty countries to prime Ted's creative juices.

The Flit contract did not prevent Ted from writing books for children, and so he worked on these between advertising projects. *The 500 Hats of Bartholomew Cubbins* (1938), *The King's Stilts* (1939), and *Horton Hatches the Egg* (1940) followed *Mulberry Street* before the United States entered World War II. Ted then took a seven-year break from writing for kids in order to contribute to the war effort.

GREAT DAY FOR FLIT!

Ted firmly believed in lucky breaks and the importance of timing. When drawing a cartoon for *Judge*, which featured a sleeping knight being annoyed by a flying dragon, Ted flipped a coin to choose between bug sprays: Flit or its rival, Fly-Tox. The wife of an advertising executive in charge of the Flit account noticed his cartoon as she was having her hair done at a salon. The woman spent two weeks nagging her husband before he finally contacted Ted. "It wasn't even her regular hairdresser," Ted later said. "He was booked that day, so she went someplace else. Her regular hairdresser was much ritzier and would never have had a copy of *Judge* in his salon."

An aerial view of Fox Studios, where Geisel
was assigned to work while serving in the army
during World War II.

Chapter 3
IF I RAN THE STUDIO

In the fall of 1942, Ted was offered an army commission as a captain. He had already joined the war effort as a civilian, drawing cartoons for *PM Magazine* in support of President Franklin Delano Roosevelt, and creating posters for the War Production Board and the Treasury Department. Like most events in Ted's life, his experience in the army was a platform for his unique artistic talent. Captain Geisel was assigned to Fort Fox, as in Hollywood's Fox Studios, to make training films for U.S. troops. He served under Major Frank Capra, an Academy Award-winning director and producer.

Ted's cohorts included composers, illustrators, screenwriters, producers, novelists, and animators (notably Warner Brothers' Chuck Jones and Friz Freleng). Ted wore a custom-made Brooks Brothers uniform and completed drills, but instead of sleeping in barracks, he returned each night to the home he shared with Helen on Wonderview Drive in the Hollywood Hills. During this time, Helen wrote children's books under her maiden name, Palmer, for Golden Books and Disney. "She supported us during the war," Ted said.

OH, TO POACH FROM FORT ROACH!

During World War II, air force personnel were stationed at the Hal Roach Studios in Culver City, California. When Ted was casting the narrator for *Your Job in Germany*, he auditioned two actors from "Fort Roach," Sergeant John Beal and Lieutenant Ronald Reagan. Beal had played lead roles in such films as *The Man Who Found Himself*, and shared billing with Katherine Hepburn in *Break of Hearts* and with William Powell and Myrna Loy in *Double Wedding*. Reagan had a skimpier resume, acting mostly in "B" movies until his breakout role in *Kings Row*. Ted chose Beal to narrate, commenting years later that Reagan "didn't seem to have the understanding, that morning, of the vital issues." Lieutenant Ronald Regan would later be elected president of the United States in 1980.

From Frank Capra and Jack Jones, animator of Bugs Bunny and Daffy Duck, Ted learned how to write scripts concisely and how to advance the plot. From Chuck Jones, young master animator and future lifelong friend, Ted learned about the art of animation. Often Ted and other Fort Fox soldiers took lunch breaks in restaurants at the Farmers' Market, what they considered their "commissary," near Beverly Hills.

Along with illustrator P. D. Eastman, Ted worked on a cartoon series featuring Private Snafu, a goofy recruit who thought he knew best how to run the army. Ted wrote verse for *Gripes*, a cartoon in the series about KP (kitchen patrol) duty, and with Chuck Jones he created *Spies*, a cartoon about avoiding talk that would tip off enemy forces. With Major W. Munro Leaf (who wrote *The Story of Ferdinand*), Ted adapted a script on a series about Ann, the Anopheles mosquito that spread malaria to U.S. troops.

As his screenwriting skills increased, Ted, now forty, was promoted to Major. He began to work with Chuck Jones on a feature length propaganda film, *Your Job in Germany*, for U.S. troops who would occupy Germany after the war. As writer and producer, Ted traveled throughout Europe to screen the film for U.S. generals at the front and behind enemy lines. After the war, the film was remade into *Hitler Lives?*, which won the Academy Award for Best Documentary Short Subject in 1946 for Warner Brothers. However,

Ann the Anopheles mosquito was a character Geisel created to help inform American troops of the dangers of malaria.

Ted received no credit. Germany surrendered sixteen days after the original film was released, and Ted's next project became *Our Job in Japan*. Japan surrendered in August 1945.

Back in Springfield, just one month later, Ted's older sister, Marnie, died suddenly of a heart condition at the age of forty-three. Devastated, Ted was unable to discuss this loss with anyone for the rest of his life.

Ted left active duty early in 1946 as a lieutenant colonel. He was awarded the Legion of Merit for "exceptionally meritorious service in planning and producing films, particularly those utilizing animated cartoons, for training, informing, and enhancing the morale of troops." After the war, Warner Brothers producer Jerry Wald hired Ted at $500 (worth about $6,000 in today's U.S. dollars) a week to work on studio projects, including *Rebel Without a Cause*. Ted's offbeat, independent style of creativity was not a good match for the culture of Hollywood screenwriters, however, and he later backed out of the agreement. Then RKO offered Ted the chance to adapt *Our Job in Japan*, which, after thirty-two revisions, was released by RKO as *Design for Death*. This forty-eight minute film won an Oscar for Best Documentary Feature of 1947.

After closing their wartime Hollywood Hills home, the Geisels spent the summer of 1946 at a friend's villa overlooking the Pacific. Loving the West Coast climate, Ted was determined to spend the rest of his life being able to "walk around outside in my pajamas." Inspired by the sunlight and the water, Ted began to paint illustrations for his first children's book in seven years,

McElligot's Pool, in brilliant blues and greens teeming with fabulously odd aquatic creatures. Featuring Marco from *Mulberry Street* who caught no fish but dreamt of an undersea adventure, the book earned Ted's first Caldecott citation and was a Junior Literary Guild selection, both prestigious awards in children's publishing.

The Geisels bought a parcel of land with an old observation tower and built a hilltop home overlooking the city of La Jolla. The Tower was Ted's retreat and studio for the rest of his life. *Thidwick the Big-Hearted Moose* was published in 1948 and became another Junior Literary Guild selection.

The following year, Bartholomew Cubbins made a comeback from the 500 hats with *Bartholomew and the Oobleck*, a tale about a king who complained about every kind of weather. The story was inspired by complaints overheard by Ted in Belgium during the war: "I didn't dream it up." Two American soldiers stuck behind enemy lines in the Battle of the Bulge with Ted were sick of rain. They complained, "Rain, always rain! Why can't we have something different for a change?" Something different was definitely in the air for Ted's career, as the mid-century approached.

Gerald McBoing Boing, based on an original story Ted had sold to Capital Records in 1950, featured a wordless boy who speaks through many different sound effects. United Productions of America (UPA) developed it as a cartoon and it won the 1951 Academy Award for Animated Short Film. *If I Ran the Zoo* (1950) followed, and then Hollywood beckoned again when Ted's fantasy film, *The 5,000 Fingers of Dr. T*, was approved in 1951. The plot is pure Seuss: A boy escapes his dreaded piano lessons in a dream that pits him against an evil music teacher who has enslaved 500 students in a musical torture chamber. The production was a debacle, however, and Ted called the night of the sneak preview in Los Angeles "the worst evening of my life... At the end there were only five people left besides [producer Stanley] Kramer and our staff. It was a disaster. Careers were ruined."

Despite the poor showing of *The 5,000 Fingers of Dr. T*, Ted's career as a children's author was still skyrocketing. After *Dr. T* finished shooting, Ted rushed his tenth book, *Scrambled Eggs*

The film adaptation of The 5,000 Fingers of Dr. T was not well received by audiences or critics, but Geisel's reputation as an author and illustrator continued to grow.

Super!, to his editor at Random House. He continued writing children's stories for magazines, from *Redbook* to the *Junior Catholic Messenger*, while furthering the adventures of Marco, Horton, and Bartholomew, and producing stories and characters that he would later work into books, such as *The Sneetches*. That same year, a *Life* magazine article by John Hersey caught Ted's attention. Hersey criticized the dull Dick-and-Jane readers of the day, saying Dr. Seuss could do a better job writing books for beginners.

As Ted was pondering this new direction of his talents, Helen developed a near-fatal illness in 1954 that required months of hospitalization and rehabilitation therapy. Ted was lost without his companion, business manager, and editor. He stayed by her side and encouraged her during her slow crawl back from paralysis and mental confusion. For the rest of her life Helen was never free from daily pain or periods of fatigue and depression.

With the crisis over, the Geisels resumed their routine at the Tower. In 1955, Ted was given an honorary doctorate from his alma mater, Dartmouth, making him an official "Doctor" Seuss. Ted's art was still in demand in the advertising world, and many of his fantastic creatures appeared on posters, billboards, and subway cards for the Holly Sugar Corporation from 1955 to 1957.

The "Doctor" with some of his fantastic creatures.

METER MATTERS

Ted's mastery of rhyme and meter made his books memorable and appealing to adults and kids alike. There are many different kinds of meter. William Shakespeare, for example, used a common kind of meter called iambic pentameter. The particular kind of meter used in most of Dr. Seuss's books is known as "anapestic tetrameter." Each line of a poem using this kind of meter has four "anapests." Each anapest is made up of four rhythmic meters composed of two weak syllables followed by a beat of one strong syllable, with one first weak syllable left out, or an added weak syllable included at the end. For example, Ted used the same meter inspired by the ship's engines for *Mulberry Street* ("And *that* is a *story* that *no* one can *beat* / When I *say* that I *saw* it on *Mulberry Street*") and for *Yertle the Turtle* ("And to*day* the Great *Yertle*, that *Marvelous* he / Is *King* of the *Mud*. That is all he can *see*"). Another meter he used was "trochaic tetrameter," with a strong syllable followed by a weak syllable, like this: ("*One* Fish/*Two* Fish/*Red* Fish/*Blue* Fish").

Ted returned to the idea of creating a book for beginning readers. Scanning a list of 223 easy-to-read words he received from his publisher, Ted noticed that "cat" and "hat" was the first rhyming pair of words. Just like that, a classic book character, and the logo for Random House's new Beginner Books imprint, made his debut: the Cat in the Hat.

Ted Geisel was known for his lighthearted personality. Here, he sketches his friend, editor Clifton Fadiman, as the Cat in the Hat.

Chapter 4
MAKING STRUDEL WITHOUT THE STRUDELS

As television and comic books lured youngsters away from books, publishers and educators brainstormed about ways to get them back. Director of Houghton Mifflin's education division, William Spaulding, challenged Ted over a business dinner in Boston to "Write… a story that first graders can't put down!" Ted and his friend and editor at Random House, Bennett Cerf, rose to the challenge. They agreed to give Houghton Mifflin rights to the school edition while retaining the trade edition. Now all Ted needed was a book.

For more than seven frustrating months Ted played with the list of beginner vocabulary words: "There are no adjectives!" he complained. He tried to write a story about a bird, without using the word "bird" (not on the list). He could use "wing thing," and "fly," but not "tail" or "eggs." "I solved my problem by writing *The Cat in the Hat*. How I did it is no trade secret. The method is the same method you use when you sit down to make apple strudel without the strudels."

The Cat in the Hat was a smash hit in 1957. Incredibly, *How the Grinch Stole Christmas!* was published during that same magical

Geisel working on sketches for *How the Grinch Stole Christmas!*

year, followed a year later by *The Cat in the Hat Comes Back*. Basking in this success, Random House launched a new division for early readers, called Beginner Books, and took the Cat in the Hat as its mascot. Ted ran the imprint as president, with Helen and Bennett Cerf's wife, Phyllis, as business partners. Together, the three would make decisions about which books their company would publish. The company negotiated a contract with Grolier Children's Book Club for sales of Beginner Books reprints, becoming the club with the longest-running, biggest sales (forty million dollars in royalties).

The Geisels worked mostly from their West Coast home in the Tower, but they also visited the Beginner Books offices tucked away on the top floor of Random House's mansion headquarters. Ted and

Phyllis often argued about everything from authors and illustrators to where to put a comma on a page. Ted and Helen considered P. D. Eastman's *Sam and the Firefly* inferior work and wanted to reject it, but they lost the battle when partner Phyllis used her influence at the New York office. Ted and Helen also did not like Random House authors Mae and Ira Freeman's *You Will Go to the Moon*, with its "lunk-headed child" who gets to the Moon but "practically immediately goes to bed." Like *Sam and the Firefly*, though, it went on to be published as a Beginner Book. Ted's Dartmouth classmate Mike McClintock created *A Fly Went By* for the imprint twenty years after he met Ted on Madison Avenue and gave him a contract for *Mulberry Street*. Helen's title, *A Fish Out of Water*, based on Ted's 1950 story for *Redbook*, "Gustave the Goldfish," joined the imprint's growing list of books.

Another legendary Seuss success resulted when Bennett Cerf bet Ted $50 that he could not write a book using just fifty beginner words. Ted won the bet in 1960 using just forty-nine in *Green Eggs and Ham*. This was the same year Beginner Books launched P. D. Eastman's *Are You My Mother?* and Robert Lopshire's *Put Me In the Zoo*.

Each time Ted delivered a new book to his publisher, a memo circulated to the staff announcing the visit and a reading by the author himself. Ted's booming voice as he recited his rhymes must have been inspirational and thrilling. Sometimes when he finished reading, Ted would ask someone else to read his words as he watched the reaction of the Random House associates.

While running Beginner Books, Ted created early readers such as *Hop on Pop*, *Dr. Seuss's ABC* (1963), and *Fox in Socks* (1965), as well as his "big books," including *Dr. Seuss's Sleep Book* (1962) and *I Had Trouble in Getting to Solla Sollew* (1965). Ted and Helen guided friends Marge and Fred Phleger on their Beginner Books titles, *The Whales Go By* and *You Will Live Under the Sea*. Ted was demanding of his authors, holding them to standards as high as his own regarding text (describe only what is pictured) and illustrations (include only one per page). Many authors who couldn't work with Ted's rules moved to other publishers. One team who stuck with Ted was Jan and Stan Berenstain. Ted liked their bear drawings and named the popular series *The Berenstain Bears*.

Around this time, war-time buddy and animator Chuck Jones convinced Ted that the Grinch was a perfect character for a TV special. With Ted as co-producer, Jones worked on storyboards while Ted wrote lyrics for "The Grinch Song" and "Welcome Christmas." Boris Karloff, famous for his roles in many horror movies, including *Frankenstein* (1931), voiced the Grinch. Finding a sponsor for the special was not as easy, however. Companies like Kellogg's and Nestlé passed, but finally the Foundation for Commercial Banks agreed. As cartoon animator and book artist, Jones and Ted clashed. Jones thought the Grinch should have green eyes, rather than pink, as in the book. Ted disagreed, but Jones prevailed. CBS aired the show on December 18, 1966, and it soon took its place among holiday classics like *A Charlie Brown Christmas* and *A Christmas Carol*.

Flush with the success of the *Grinch* TV special, Jones and Ted started work on adapting *Horton Hears a Who!* While working on this follow up to the *Grinch*, Ted's wife Helen passed away suddenly in October of 1967. Ted was stunned with grief.

Ted retreated to his studio that winter and worked on *The Foot Book*, the first in the new Bright & Early pre-reader series. In summer 1968, he married longtime friend Audrey Dimond.

Audrey's daughters from her first marriage, Lark and Lea Grey, (whom Ted called "Lee Groo") came to live at the Tower when they were not away at boarding school. As Audrey joined Ted in his personal and professional adventures, more Beginner Books and Bright & Early Books emerged from the San Diego studio: *My Book About Me*; *Mr. Brown Can Moo, Can You?*; and *The Lorax*, a cautionary tale about pollution.

To break from the demands of running Beginner Books, Ted often wrote as Theo LeSieg (Geisel spelled backward) with others illustrating. By age seventy-five, Ted was battling eye problems. His Beginner Book, *I Can Read With My Eyes Shut!* was dedicated to his eye specialist, David Worthen, E. G. (Eye Guy). In an interview with the *Los Angeles Times Book Review* around this time he stated that "I tend to exaggerate in life, and in writing, it's fine to exaggerate... For another thing, writing is easier than digging ditches. Well, actually, that's an exaggeration. It isn't."

Ted Geisel with his second wife, Audrey, and the Cat in the Hat in 1981.

Chapter 5
OH, THE PLACES TED GOES!

At age seventy-nine, Ted started treatment for a type of cancer discovered under his tongue. Despite the bad news, he continued work on *The Butter Battle Book*. The book is about two camps of creatures, the Yooks and the Zooks, who disagree about how to eat their buttered toast. The two begin building increasingly extraordinary and powerful weapons to support their side, threatening to destroy both sides in the process. Many people read the *Butter Battle Book* as a parable for the nuclear arms race between the U.S. and Russia at the time.

In 1980, Ted was awarded the Laura Ingalls Wilder Medal from professional children's librarians. In 1984, he received a Pulitzer citation for his contribution to children's literature. Ted told an interviewer that year, "I feel my greatest accomplishment was getting rid of Dick and Jane and encouraging students to approach reading as a pleasure, not a chore."

Ted's experience as a reluctant medical patient led to *You're Only Old Once! A Book for Obsolete Children* in 1986 and his final book in 1990, *Oh, the Places You'll Go!*. His friends at Random

House realized that this was probably the last Dr. Seuss book and did not assume that Ted would arrive with the usual celebratory staff reading. The book became a *New York Times* bestseller and popular gift for "upstarts of all ages," selling well to people who gift the book, often to graduates of high school and college. In June 1991, *Six by Seuss: A Treasury of Dr. Seuss Classics* became a main selection of the Book-of-the-Month Club.

That summer, Ted's health continued to fail. In what would be his last interview, he was asked if he had left anything unsaid in his books. Ted gave biographers Judith and Neil Morgan a message for his readers: "Whenever things go a bit sour in a job I'm doing, I always tell myself, 'You can do better than this.' ...We can and we've got to... do better than this." Throughout the fall, Ted continued to talk with his family and doctors, in and out of consciousness. He offered Theophrastus, the brown dog he had held close since childhood, to Audrey's daughter, Lea Grey, saying, "You will take care of the dog, won't you?" On September 24, 1991, Ted passed away at the age of eighty-seven.

Audrey continued to oversee the Dr. Seuss global enterprise as president and CEO. Despite their creator's passing, many of Dr. Seuss's creations continued to come to life. The 2000-2001 Broadway show *Seussical* toured nationally. The 2000 film version of *How the Grinch Stole Christmas*, starring Jim Carrey, was a box office smash, grossing $260 million domestically. *The Cat in the Hat* was also adapted for movie screens in 2003 and featured Mike Myers as the cat of Seuss's classic book.

Dr. Seuss and his characters are forever remembered in this sculpture garden in his hometown, Springfield.

In 2002, Ted was immortalized in his hometown with the opening of the Dr. Seuss National Memorial Sculpture Garden in Springfield, Massachusetts. The park features bronze sculptures created by Lark Grey Dimond-Cates, Ted's stepdaughter.

At the quadrangle near the Springfield Library in the heart of Ted's hometown sits a fourteen-foot Horton the Elephant, along with sculptures of Thing One and Thing Two, the Grinch and his dog, Max, and Dr. Seuss at his drawing board with the Cat in the Hat posing nearby. Other Seussian figures (the Lorax, Yertle the Turtle, Thidwick the Big-Hearted Moose, and

Seuss Landing in
Orlando, Florida.

others) fill the city's quadrangle, as well.

In Orlando, Florida, families can visit Seuss Landing at Universal's Islands of Adventure theme park and hop on the Caro-Seuss-el or the High in the Sky Seuss Trolley Train Ride. On the other side of the United States, visitors can see the Dr. Seuss star on the Hollywood Walk of Fame at the 6500 block of Hollywood Boulevard.

In 2004, the Association for Library Service to Children established the annual Theodor Seuss Geisel Award to honor the "most distinguished American book for beginning readers" for years pre-K to grade two.

The PBS television series, *The Cat in the Hat Knows a Lot About That!,* began in 2010. Random House Children's Books released *The Bippolo Seed and Other Lost Stories*, a new collection of old treasures, in 2011. These seven stories were published in magazines during the 1950s and show how elements of Ted's characters and plots evolved.

Also in 2011, Illumination Entertainment and actor Johnny Depp's Infinitum Nihil production company announced that they were developing a movie about the life of Dr. Seuss, to be distributed by Universal Pictures. Depp will produce the movie and possibly star as Ted Geisel himself. Universal released a CGI-animated adaptation of *The Lorax* on March 2, 2012, the 108th anniversary of Ted's birth.

Ted Geisel never thought of himself as a "kid's author." He wrote and illustrated to please himself, and was delighted that children and adults alike enjoyed his books. "I never had a desire to save the world," he said. "My desire was simply to say something and express myself; to stimulate the brain cells of my readers and teach children something vitally important: to understand and appreciate the value of reading."

SELECTED BOOKS BY DR. SEUSS

DR. SEUSS "BIG BOOKS"

And to Think That I Saw It on Mulberry Street (1937)

The 500 Hats of Bartholomew Cubbins (1938)

Horton Hatches the Egg (1940)

McElligot's Pool (1947) (Caldecott Honor Book)

Bartholomew and the Oobleck (1949) (Caldecott Honor Book)

If I Ran the Zoo (1950) (Caldecott Honor Book)

Horton Hears a Who! (1954)

If I Ran the Circus (1955)

How the Grinch Stole Christmas! (1957)

The Sneetches and Other Stories (1961)

The Lorax (1971) (NCSS Notable Children's Trade Book)

The Butter Battle Book (1984)

Oh, the Places You'll Go! (1990)

BEGINNER BOOKS

The Cat in the Hat (1957)

The Cat in the Hat Comes Back (1958)

One Fish Two Fish Red Fish Blue Fish (1960)

Green Eggs and Ham (1960)

Hop on Pop (1963)

Oh, the Thinks You Can Think! (1975)

BRIGHT & EARLY BOOKS

Oh, Say Can You Say? (1979)

aquatic—living or growing in water

bootleg—made or sold illegally

brewery—plant where malt liquor (beer) is produced

debacle—failure, disaster

GI—a name for a soldier in the U.S. army, especially during World War II

imprint—a brand name of books published by a larger company

meandered—wandered casually

menagerie—a collection of animals

meter—the rhythm of a line of poetry

nostalgia—fond feelings about a past event or experience

Prohibition—law forbidding the manufacture, transport, and sale of alcohol

propaganda—information, usually biased or misleading, spread to influence the public

prototypes—a first model from which later forms are made

pseudonyms—false or pen names

vaudeville—a type of entertainment popular in the 20th century that featured a variety of acts, including comedy and song and dance

Yankee—used to describe people from the northern part of the U.S., especially New England

CHRONOLOGY

March 2, 1904: Theodor Seuss Geisel is born in Springfield, Massachusetts.

1918: Joining the World War I war effort, Ted sells war bonds and grows a victory garden.

1920: The Geisel family beer business crumbles as Prohibition begins.

1921: Ted enters college at Dartmouth as an English major.

1925: Ted attends Oxford University to pursue post-graduate studies.

1927: Helen Palmer and Ted Geisel marry in November.

1928: The successful Flit bug spray ads begin, making it possible for the Geisels to move to a better apartment and travel extensively.

1936: Ted writes his first children's book, *And to Think That I Saw It on Mulberry Street*.

1942: Ted accepts an army commission and makes training films for troops at Fort Fox in Hollywood.

1954: Helen is diagnosed with Guillain-Barré syndrome.

1957: Based on the success of *The Cat in the Hat*, Random House launches the Beginner Books imprint.

1960: Ted writes *Green Eggs and Ham* using less than fifty words, winning a $50 bet with his editor.

1966: *How the Grinch Stole Christmas!* airs on CBS in December and eventually becomes a holiday classic.

1967: Helen Geisel passes away suddenly.

1968: Ted and Audrey Stone Dimond are married.

1975: After a cancer diagnosis, Ted begins treatment.

1980: Children's librarians award Ted the Laura Ingalls Wilder Medal.

1991: Ted dies at home on September 24.

FURTHER INFORMATION

Books

Levine, Gail Carson. *Writing Magic*. New York, NY: HarperCollins, 2006.

Messner, Kate. *Real Revision: Authors' Strategies to Share with Student Writers*. Portland, ME: Stenhouse, 2011.

Websites

Dr. Seuss Biography

www.drseussart.com/biography.html

Read a detailed biography of Dr. Seuss' life, discover answers to frequently asked questions, and explore the art of Dr. Seuss.

Dr. Seuss National Memorial Sculpture Garden at the Springfield Museums

www.catinthehat.org/history.htm

The official website of the Springfield, Massachusetts, memorial for Dr. Seuss features a brief biography, pictures of some of the memorial sculptures, and updates about events.

Dr. Seuss's Website

www.seussville.com

At Dr. Seuss' website, you can explore a virtual studio, play games, watch videos, and more.

BIBLIOGRAPHY

A note to report writers

To write this biography, I reread many of Dr. Seuss's books and did research online, reading articles that had been written about Ted Geisel by other journalists. I also read books about Ted's career. Below is a list of sources I used. Any time you write a report, you should also keep track of where you got your information from. It is fine to use information in your report that you found somewhere else, as long as you give the source credit in a footnote, endnote, or within the report itself. (Your teacher can tell you how he or she prefers you list your sources.) It is not fine to pass off other people's work as your own.

BOOKS

Cohen, Charles D. *The Seuss, the Whole Seuss, and Nothing But the Seuss*. New York, NY: Random House, 2004.

Morgan, Judith and Neil. *Dr. Seuss and Mr. Geisel*. New York, NY: Da Capo Press, 1995.

Pease, Donald E. *Theodor Seuss Geisel*. New York, NY: Oxford University Press, 2010.

PERIODICALS

Corwin, Miles and Tom Gorman. "Theodor Geisel Dies at 87: Wrote 47 Dr. Seuss Books." *LA Times*, September 26, 1991.

Lamothe, Ron. "PBS Independent Lens: The Political Dr. Seuss." *The Washington Post*, October 27, 2004.

Pace, Eric. "Dr. Seuss, Modern Mother Goose, Dies at 87." *New York Times*, September 26, 1991.

ONLINE

"Celebrating Dr. Seuss." Joy Bean, http://www.publishersweekly.com/pw/print/20040202/21683-celebrating-dr-seuss.html

"Dr. Seuss—Hollywood Star Walk." Miles Corwin and Tom Gorman, http://projects.latimes.com/hollywood/star-walk/dr-seuss/

"Johnny Depp to Become Dr. Seuss for Illumination and Universal." Borys Kit, Jay A. Fernandez, www.hollywoodreporter.com/risky-business/johnny-depp-dr-seuss-universal-illumination-245072

"Seussentennial: 100 Years of Dr. Seuss." Associated Press, http://www.today.com/id/4362025#.UvKTh7T6SRM

"Theodore Seuss Geisel: Author Study." Melissa Kaplan, www.anapsid.org/aboutmk/seuss.html

INDEX

ABOUT THE AUTHOR:

Deborah Grahame-Smith is a writer and editor who has worked for children's book publishers including Scholastic, Millbrook Press, and Cavendish Square. She is also the author of several nonfiction books for kids. A native of Long Island, New York, she lives in Connecticut.